Pray Attention

Pray Attention

5 SACRED MEDITATIONS
with Audio

Diane Scribner Clevenger

O'LEARY PUBLISHING
The Influencer's Press

BONITA SPRINGS, FL

Copyright © 2020 by Pray Attention Ministries

All rights reserved.

Published in the United States by
O'Leary Publishing
www.olearypublishing.com

The views, information, or opinions expressed in this book are solely those of the authors involved and do not necessarily represent those of O'Leary Publishing, LLC.

ISBN: 978-1-7341589-0-8 (print)
ISBN: 978-1-7337104-9-7 (ebook)
Library of Congress Control Number: 2019916295

Cover Design by Christine Dupre
Interior Design by Jessica Angerstein

Printed in the United States of America

This book is dedicated to my beloved sons,
Justin and Garen

Contents

Intro
1

Meditation 1
Your Regenerating Heart
3

Meditation 2
Sweet Surrender
23

Meditation 3
Feel the Touch
39

Meditation 4
Allow God to be God in You
59

Meditation 5
The Divine Plan Unfolding
79

Outro
97

Before you start

Download the Digital Audio Tracks:
prayattentionministries.org/download

OR

Purchase the Companion Audio CD:
prayattentionministries.org/products

Intro

~ START AUDIO TRACK NOW ~

Welcome to Pray Attention. I'm Diane Scribner Clevenger and I'll be guiding you on this journey.

This book contains 5 Sacred Meditations, for you to rejuvenate, relax, and reconnect with yourself.

I encourage you to follow along in this booklet, by yourself or with someone you love. Contemplate the words. Let them sink into your soul.

Listening to the companion audio and reading 5 Sacred Meditations, is a perfect way to introduce children to the skillful practice of meditation. Allow them to hold the booklet and follow along with the words, perhaps pointing to the words as I say them.

Another idea is to share this with other adults in your life. You may want to sit down with them to listen, read, and be still together.

I encourage you to create time and space in your busy schedule to slow down and enjoy at least one Sacred Meditation each day.

Come with me now, and let's Pray Attention together...

Your Regenerating Heart

Here we are, Lord…

I invite you to take a long, slow, deep breath as we begin this time of prayer and meditation together.

As you breathe in, breathe in the grace of God. And as you breathe out, let go all that may concern you.

Place it firmly in God's hands.

Breathe, beloved.

And as you deepen your breath, you may feel that you are sinking into your chair. Allow your *self* to do so.

Completely relax. For this temple you are in is the holy temple of God – yours, to just allow…

This is God time. Let every part of you feel at peace.

The Presence of God is here, around you now, within you, moving through you.

As you breathe in and as you breathe out, feel the mighty current and power that sustains you, revives you, regenerates you and is nourishing you now…

Let every breath be an opportunity to feel this Presence of God - Pure Spirit.

Visualize, if you will, a cleansing white Light around your heart space. It is blessing you.

This Light moves from your heart to every part of your body as Life Force, as God Essence. And, if, in this time, there is any place that needs support,

Allow and encourage this Light to go there, now.

Breathe into this Light…

In this time, you are filled to overflowing – allow this beautiful, golden-white Light to move now beyond your individual body to others – those you would have accept their healing.

Feel the increasing range of your light as it permeates those around you in your spiritual community, in your family, in all your relations – radiating to those who may not be present in the room with you, those dear to you and those not yet known to you.

What a blessing…

(break in music & speaking on audio track)

See, in your mind's eye, this light filling their hearts, their bodies, all their circumstances with grace and nourishing them with God's embracing love.

Relax even more deeply now and please allow my words to become as your inner thoughts -

Oh Holy Presence, how grateful I am that You are here, now, in me. My search has been to find God where I am and I find You in my world.

I find Spirit in all things for, truly, back of any fear or doubt or uncertainty I have ever had, there has been a great assurance.

May that wisdom rise up in me. May I know that as my foundation.

That after the flood, there is dry land, and I do begin again.

That after my wandering, feeling lost, I find that I have never been alone - for You have been with me and I in You…

Oh, God – my God – You are my life.

I am not attaining a God-filled life for your kingdom is my very breath. It is the ground upon which I walk, the word I speak, the actions I take.

I cannot be separated from my Essential Self.

And so, here, in this time of prayer, I no longer struggle to find, but to accept.

And as I accept Your Presence, everything in me that I ever limited with my own beliefs flow together, it rushes together as a mountain torrent rushes across the valley to join the vast ocean – You in me and I in You.

I am so grateful to be here with You, sweet, sweet Spirit.

I hold You in my heart in silence now as I follow Your breath breathing me, giving and receiving, giving and receiving, in silence…

> (break in music & speaking on audio track)

For this breath, for this prayer time, for the capacity to bless and feel Your Presence, dear Lord, for all this and so much more, I am grateful to Thee.

Have Your Way with me, Lord.

Amen.

Ideas to **Pray Attention** to...

Ideas to **Pray** *Attention to...*

Ideas to **Pray Attention** *to...*

Ideas to **Pray Attention** *to...*

Ideas to **Pray
Attention** *to...*

Sweet Surrender

Beloved, let us rest awhile…

Allow your body temple to become very still.

Relax…

Apart from the things of the world, this is your time to retreat to that place of stillness that indwells you.

Listen, in this time, to the words of Lowell Fillmore:

"When for a purpose I had prayed and prayed and prayed until my words seemed worn and bare with arduous use, and I had knocked and asked and knocked and asked again, and all my fervor and persistence brought no hope, I paused to give my weary brain a rest and ceased my anxious human cry.

In that still moment, after self had tried and failed, there came a glorious vision of God's power, and, lo, my prayer was answered in that hour."[1]

---

1 from the poem, The Answer

This is your time to give it up to God.

Whatever has been on your mind,
in your heart, give it up to God.

In this time of sweet surrender, you can hold the light of the Lord before you,

And into that light pour all your concerns…

This is your time to commit and to dedicate and to surrender to the glorious Power that is greater than you alone.

Oh, yes, you are so connected to the network of this Universe that you can rise on wings of freedom by simply giving it all to the Lord of your Being.

Give up now, the names of those whom you have tightly in your mind.

Any doubts, any worries – place them firmly now in God's hands for this is your place of answer, your place of peace.

Be still and know.

Be still and know…

(break in music & speaking on audio track)

Precious Spirit,
Sweet Presence,
I thank You.

How delightful it is to go into the quiet zone, with You.

You indwell me.

I am You and You are the active Power and Presence in me.

Carry me forth now, Lord, to do Your work, to live in Your way.

Would that each choice would be aligned with that Power - that absolute Presence and Assurance with which You energize me.

This day proclaimed in Christ's name.

Amen.

Ideas to **Pray**
*A***ttention** to...

Ideas to **Pray** *Attention to...*

Ideas to **Pray Attention** *to...*

Ideas to **Pray** *A***ttention** *to...*

Ideas to **Pray Attention** *to...*

Feel the Touch

Feel the touch of the Divine.

Lift your *self* now, in this moment,

From any sense of outer confusion
to inner peace, from turmoil to tranquility.

Do not try so hard, my beloved.

Allow your human mind to step aside, for this is a time when there is no need of word or deed - this is a time with the God of your Being.

Spirit has words to give you, living words
of Truth. They shall guide you and light
your path.

And, you – you must be open to
your consciousness, to the very highest that
you are here to receive of God.

To no other source need you ever look
for inspiration, for the Lord of your being is
your completeness and supplies every need.

There have been times when outer help seems to have been taken from you. Know now, it is only that you may come to recognize from whence comes your supply.

This lesson is very necessary for you in order that you may be fitted to carry out your work, your unique service – here, in this life-wave.

Could some human vessel bring you more wisdom than the Beloved of your soul?

This is a time of quiet meditation.

Breathe…

Relax…

For the way is always made clear.

Ease into the hearing of my voice –

My direction, my guidance are for you.

Within the center of your being, where Spirit dwells.

There are no fears.

All is calm, sure.

Here, harmony will always prevail.

Come now…

You do know.

> (break in music & speaking on audio track of 1+ minute)

For I have taught you that if, and when, you abide with Me in the consciousness of my Presence – at the heart, the center of your life – all confusion shall give way to a great, eternal peace.

Then, with what sureness shall you go about your daily work, knowing that the pattern of your life is being worked out according to the design planned by life's great architect.

And I shall give you lessons, and you shall learn.

Allow your *self* the time…

Give your *self* the gift of accepting the Truth. It is here. Take these truths into your heart that they may work for you –

For they are not only to be heard, but used as a pattern for your daily living. And, unless they are made so, what help are the lessons?

Spirit loves you so completely, longs for you to feel the glory and the presence and grace - that there is no other way possible.

Hear that,

Feel that…

The Touch of the Divine in you, in tranquility now, come before the God of your Being. Receive.

Listen…

Ideas to **Pray** *A***ttention** *to...*

Ideas to **Pray Attention** *to...*

Ideas to **Pray Attention** *to...*

Ideas to **Pray**
*A***ttention** *to...*

Allow God to be God in You

Welcome.

Welcome, into this time of quiet.

Time to rise on wings of freedom, as you draw nigh unto your inner *Self*.

This is a time of intention. A time to set apart all of the doingness of the world.

There is nothing you need do except to allow your *self* to go where God would lead you - as you allow God to be God in you.

And so, relax.

Breathe deeply of the abundant air all around you -

It is freely given and so freely now, receive.

Be still…

Your soul is profound in its capacity to receive. And in times such as this, when all else is set aside, ah, there is your God essence.

If the cask is to contain wine, you must first pour out the water.

It must be bare, it must be empty, and, therefore, ready.

You are here to receive divine joy,
the goodness of Spirit. So, pour out now,
anything you may feel you are clinging to –
expectations, concerns, fears.

See them floating as if on a river…

You will deal with them in God-time.

Let them float now...

Beloved, in this time of prayer, know that you cannot obtain more of God, by contemplation or pious devotion or religious retreat, than by being at the fireplace, or by working in the stable, or by sitting now in quiet…

(break in music & talking on audio track)

Your silence is a natural state of Being.

It points you toward God, just as every creature, every experience, leads you toward new birth and toward seeing the world as God sees it – transparently.

What a delight, it is, to come into a calm state, where gratitude rises in our hearts.

Where we can count our blessings and know that You are the one Presence and the one Power, and for having taken this time when we can pour all of our worldly knowing, all of our unknowing, all of the potentialities, and all of the possibilities into Your Mightiness.

For this we say, Thank You God.

For this Is the Assurance, that day to day reminds us – moment to moment helps us remember – that we are Your divine, beloved children, here, entrusted with one another as we rise on wings of freedom this day.

And for this we say, Thank You God.

In Christ's name.

Amen.

Ideas to **Pray Attention** to...

Ideas to **Pray Attention** *to...*

Ideas to **Pray
*A*ttention** *to...*

Ideas to **Pray** *A***ttention** *to...*

Ideas to **Pray**
*A***ttention** *to...*

The Divine Plan Unfolding

Welcome.

Welcome, my beloved,

As you come quietly now into this space of mediation and prayer.

For this is apparently what you need.

Allow, in this time, a simple resting in my love and a drinking in of my peace, as you allow my words to be as the voice of Spirit within you.

Just relax and come close that I may enfold you.

Put aside all thoughts of confusion, any questions you may have. Give them unto Me - that in this resting, you and I might allow the very highest outcome to come forth in a natural and easy way.

Let's allow the Divine Plan to flow - through you, and all your affairs.

Truly, only those who love, and understand,
can flow in their own consciousness with
a love so great that it overflows to others.
And, in this way, we redeem our world.

And so quietly now, be faithful and steadfast in your meditation and I shall show you your service – for you, as a candle lit, will know in this time, where your warmth should flow…

Ah, yes… between us, always, and moving out into the world through your hands, through your heart and your thoughts and your actions, the whole world is warmed in your Light.

So, now, picturing that golden gleam of light and love that you can focus on in this time, step aside for these moments, and, resting in my Presence, you shall be able to fulfill your destiny, every place, and every time, that you are called. Incline your ear that you may receive anew the words which I would give to you.

Ah, I dwell in your heart center and no one and nothing can ever take that Holy Presence away from you.

Neither life nor death, riches nor poverty –
nothing can separate you and your Beloved.

And, so, in this time of silence, I invite you to open even further in your resting, and let go the small, personal *self* of you.

As you close the door, ever so gently, in the quiet time of our communion.

Feel the Breath - the Flow – as we quiet in stillness…

(break in music & talking on audio track)

As you come to Me,

As you blend with Me,

You – the one whom I have created –

You are awakened once again,

Invigorated once again –

By my holy presence, in you,

And in your world.

Spend time with me every day, every waking moment, and into the night, and, soon, you shall have to build a larger barn to hold your increase of Good.

I thank you for this time with Me.

I commend you, congratulate you, for, in having been in stillness, you have surely given your *self* rich gifts.

Thank you, and, thank You…

Take Me out into your world.

Take Me everywhere you go in a wakened way

Into every room,

Into every heart,

Every conversation, inner and outer.

For in this way, you lift the light of God,
so all can see...

So all can see.

Amen.

Outro

I pray this has been an enriching and enlightening time for you, as you have reconnected with your Divine Presence.

I hope you have shared your meditation practice with someone you love. To continue your journey with me, Reverend Diane, please visit us online at www.prayattentionministries.org.

Be sure to check our online calendar for upcoming events in your area. To book me for a workshop, retreat or Sunday service, or for private spiritual coaching, you can contact me through our website, and we have other programs for you to enjoy.

If you have not done so, I invite you to sign up for our free Daily Pray-It-Forward messages to quickly guide you each day, as you continue to Pray Attention to your grace-filled life.

Ideas to **Pray Attention** *to...*

Ideas to **Pray**
*A***ttention** *to...*

Ideas to **Pray Attention** *to...*

Ideas to **Pray
Attention** *to...*

Ideas to **Pray** *A*ttention *to...*

Ideas to **Pray
Attention** *to...*

www.ingramcontent.com/pod-product-compliance
Lightning Source LLC
Chambersburg PA
CBHW071359080526
44587CB00017B/3138